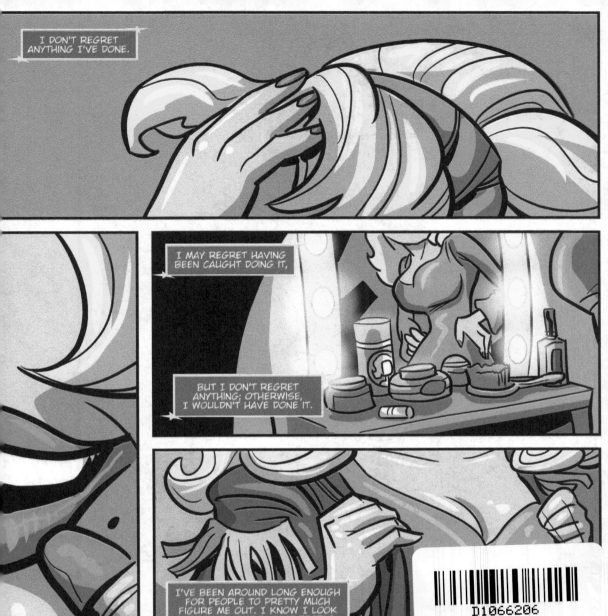

I DON'T REGRET ANYTHING I'VE DONE.

I MAY REGRET HAVING BEEN CAUGHT DOING IT,

BUT I DON'T REGRET ANYTHING; OTHERWISE, I WOULDN'T HAVE DONE IT.

I'VE BEEN AROUND LONG ENOUGH FOR PEOPLE TO PRETTY MUCH FIGURE ME OUT. I KNOW I LOOK ARTIFICIAL, BUT I WANT PEOPLE TO KNOW I'M TOTALLY REAL.

I KNOW I LOOK PHONY, BUT I'M A COUNTRY GIRL, BORN IN LOCUST RIDGE, TENNESSEE, AT HEART. BESIDES, IT COSTS A LOT OF MONEY TO LOOK THIS CHEAP.

(FORGIVE THE CRAZY BOOTS. I'M SHORT. IN ORDER TO GET TO MY CABINETS, I'VE GOTTA WEAR MY HIGH HEELS).

A LOT OF PEOPLE HAVE SAID I'D HAVE PROBABLY DONE A LOT BETTER IN MY CAREER IF I HADN'T LOOKED SO GAUDY. I DRESS TO BE COMFORTABLE FOR ME, AND YOU SHOULDN'T BE BLAMED IF YOU WANT TO LOOK PRETTY, RIGHT?

THIS STATUE, OUTSIDE THE COUNTY COURTHOUSE IN SEVIERVILLE, TENNESSEE REMINDS ME OF MY ROOTS.

DOLLY REBECCA PARTON! DON'T STARE. IT AIN'T POLITE.

MY LOOK WAS INSPIRED BY THE TOWN TRAMP. I THOUGHT SHE WAS ABSOLUTELY BEAUTIFUL BECAUSE SHE LOOKED LIKE A MOVIE STAR TO ME.

SHE HAD THOSE PILES OF BLEACHED HAIR, RED LIPSTICK, NAILS AND CHEEKS AND HIGH HEEL SHOES. BEAUTIFUL.

BESIDES, I'D NEVER STOOP SO LOW AS TO BE FASHIONABLE.

IT'S HARD TO BE A DIAMOND IN A RHINESTONE WORLD.

YOU NEED TO REALLY BELIEVE IN WHAT YOU'VE GOT TO OFFER, WHAT YOUR TALENT IS — AND IF YOU BELIEVE, THAT GIVES YOU STRENGTH.

SO UNCLE BILLY AND I STARTED KNOCKING ON DOORS AND CALLING IN FAVORS. BY THE TIME I WAS TWELVE, I APPEARED ON THE GRAND OLE OPRY THANKS TO SINGER AND SONGWRITER JIMMY C. NEWMAN. THAT CRAZY CAJUN GAVE ME HIS SPOT ON THE SHOW!

Grand Ole Opry House

BUT I WANTED MORE. WHEN I WAS SIXTEEN, UNCLE BILLY BROUGHT ME TO THE OFFICES OF TREE PUBLISHING.

WE'RE HERE TO SEE YOUR –

HE'S OUT.

NOW, WHO DID YOU THINK I –

YOU DON'T HAVE AN APPOINTMENT.

"FINE. WE'LL WAIT."

AND WE DID. ALL DAY. I THINK THEY FINALLY SAW US BECAUSE THEY WANTED TO CLOSE THE OFFICE.

THAT EVENING, UNCLE BILLY AND I SIGNED A DEAL WITH MERCURY RECORDS AND I RECORDED "IT MAY NOT KILL ME (BUT IT'S SURE GONNA HURT)" AND "I WASTED MY TEARS (WHEN I CRIED OVER YOU.)"

IF YOU HAVEN'T HAD THIS EXPERIENCE, LET ME TELL YA, IT'S A WARM FEELIN' TO HEAR YOUR MUSIC ON THE RADIO.

THAT'S ABOUT THE TIME I DECIDED THAT I NEEDED AN IMAGE MAKEOVER. A NEW LOOK. SOMETHING TO MAKE ME STAND OUT FROM THE CROWD.

I'M NO NATURAL BEAUTY. IF I'M GONNA HAVE ANY LOOKS AT ALL, I'M GONNA HAVE TO CREATE THEM.

I GOT TO FIXIN' MYSELF UP. I WANTED MY CLOTHES TIGHT, MY MAKEUP BRIGHT, MY NAILS LONG, MY LIPS RED.

NOWADAYS, IF I SEE SOMETHING SAGGIN', BAGGIN', OR DRAGGIN', I'LL GET IT NIPPED, TUCKED, OR SUCKED. BACK THEN I DIDN'T HAVE TWO DIMES TO RUB TOGETHER.

I GRADUATED HIGH SCHOOL WHEN I WAS EIGHTEEN. I ASKED MY RELATIVES FOR MONEY INSTEAD OF GIFTS.

THE NEXT DAY, I JUMPED ON A GREYHOUND BOUND FOR NASHVILLE. I WOULD'VE LEFT EARLIER, BUT DADDY WOULD'VE HUNTED ME DOWN WITH A SHOTGUN AND DRUG ME BACK TO SEVIER COUNTY. I JUST KNOW IT.

I ENDED UP HERE, IN A SMALL APARTMENT ABOVE THE WISHY WASHY LAUNDROMAT.

WISHY-WASHY
LAUNDR-O-MAT

ALL I HAD WERE MY DREAMS, MY OLD GUITAR, THE SONGS I HAD WRITTEN, AND THE REST OF MY BELONGINGS IN A SET OF MATCHING LUGGAGE—THREE PAPER BAGS FROM THE SAME GROCERY STORE.

I FIGURED I'D BE A STAR BEFORE THE MONEY RAN OUT. BUT YOU CAN'T GET SO BUSY TRYIN' TO MAKE A LIVIN' THAT YOU FORGET TO MAKE A LIFE.

WASHY
-O-MAT

HEY, BLONDIE! YOU SING LIKE AN ANGEL.

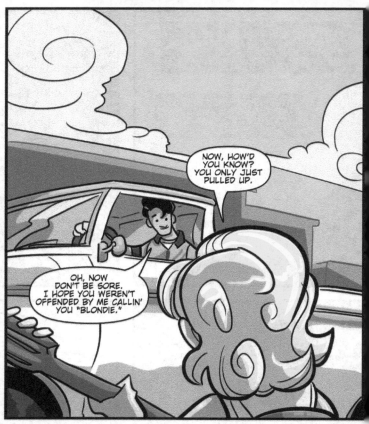

NOW, HOW'D YOU KNOW? YOU ONLY JUST PULLED UP.

OH, NOW DON'T BE SORE. I HOPE YOU WEREN'T OFFENDED BY ME CALLIN' YOU "BLONDIE."

NAW, I AIN'T OFFENDED BY THAT OR DUMB BLONDE JOKES BECAUSE I KNOW I'M NOT DUMB. AND I'M NOT BLONDE, EITHER.

TOUCHE'.

OOOO-WHEE! A FANCY TALKER.

ACTUALLY, I'VE BEEN DRIVING BY EVERY DAY TO HEAR YOU SING AND TO WORK UP THE COURAGE TO ASK YOU OUT.

HONK

C'MON! GET MOVIN'!

HOLD YER HORSES! CAN'T YOU SEE I'M ABOUT TO SCORE A DATE?

WELL, I GUESS YOU BEST COMMENCE TO ASKIN'. THE NATIVES ARE GETTING' RESTLESS. BESIDES, I GOT CLOTHES TO FOLD.

I'LL PARK AND MEET YOU INSIDE.

YOU SAID YOU'VE DRIVEN BY A FEW TIMES. WHAT MADE YOU STOP TODAY?

WELL, I WAS GOING TO SAY SOMETHING FUNNY TO GET YOU TO LAUGH, BUT I CHANGED MY MIND.

CARL THOMAS DEAN'S NOT IN SHOW BUSINESS, AND THAT'S JUST FINE WITH ME. HE'S MORE OF A LONER.

HE DOESN'T PARTICULARLY CARE ABOUT BEING AROUND ANYBODY BUT ME.

WHAT WERE YOU GONNA SAY?

HE DIDN'T HARBOR DREAMS OF LEAVING TENNESSEE OR MAKING IT BIG SOMEHOW. HE WANTED TO RUN AN ASPHALT BUSINESS AND ENJOY HIS LIFE.

I WAS GOING TO SAY, "HEY, AREN'T YOU WORRIED ABOUT GETTIN' A SUNBURN IN THAT OUTFIT?"

WHAT MAKES HIM ATTRACTIVE IS THAT HE'S SUPPORTIVE, VERY SECURE WITHIN HIMSELF, AND NOT THE JEALOUS TYPE.

HA! THAT'S HYSTERICAL! I NEVER GAVE IT MUCH THOUGHT. I RECKON I JUST WANTED TO BE COMFORTABLE.

ABOUT MY LEGIONS OF FANS, HE SAID,

"WELL, HELL, I KNOW IT'S NOT EASY OUT THERE. I'D FEEL LESS ABOUT ANY MAN THAT DIDN'T FALL IN LOVE WITH YOU."

WELL... WOULD YOU LIKE TO GO OUT TO DINNER OR SOMETHING WITH ME?

I NEED TO TELL YOU, I WAS SURPRISED AND DELIGHTED THAT THIS HANDSOME MAN LOOKED ME IN THE EYES WHEN WE WERE TALKING. THAT'S A RARE THING FOR ME.

THERE WAS ONE THING HE WAS ALWAYS SURE ABOUT:

BETTER SET ANOTHER PLATE, MA, BECAUSE THIS IS THE GIRL I'M GONNA MARRY!

AND WE DID.

ON OUR 50TH WEDDING ANNIVERSARY, HE SAID:

MY FIRST THOUGHT WAS, "I'M GONNA MARRY THAT GIRL." MY SECOND THOUGHT WAS, "LORD SHE'S GOOD LOOKIN'." AND THAT WAS THE DAY MY LIFE BEGAN.

I WOULDN'T TRADE THE LAST FIFTY YEARS FOR NOTHING ON THIS EARTH.

HE'S JUST THE FUNNIEST, WITTIEST GUY IN THE WORLD AND HE'S REALLY BRIGHT. HE'S NOT BACKWARD AT ALL, HE JUST DOESN'T HAVE ANY DESIRE TO BE IN SHOW BUSINESS,

AND HE DOESN'T WANT PEOPLE TO HAVE HIS PICTURES IN THE PAPER.

IN MY WILDEST DREAMS, I DIDN'T EXPECT THINGS TO TAKE OFF LIKE THEY DID. IT REALLY STARTED WHEN I MET PORTER WAGONER.

I REMEMBER HUDDLING IN FRONT OF THE TELEVISION TO WATCH THE PORTER WAGONER SHOW.

PORTER, "THE THIN MAN FROM WEST PLAINS, MISSOURI," HAD 29 TOP-TEN HITS DURING HIS CAREER, INCLUDING "MISERY LOVES COMPANY" AND "THE COLD HARD FACTS OF LIFE."

THE WAGON HOUSE

SOME SAY I HELPED REIGNITE HIS SIGNING AND SONGWRITING CAREER.

AT THE TIME, I WASN'T WORRIED ABOUT ALL THAT. HE PAID ME $60,000 A YEAR TO BE A VOCALIST ON HIS SHOW, AND I WAS ONLY 21 YEARS OLD. THAT'S GOOD MONEY. I PROMISED TO STAY WITH HIM FOR FIVE YEARS.

WE HAD 21 HITS TOP THE CHARTS TOGETHER AND WON THE COUNTRY MUSIC ASSOCIATION'S VOCAL DUO OF THE YEAR AWARD THREE TIMES.

BUT I ALWAYS SAY, "IF YOU DON'T LIKE THE ROAD YOU'RE WALKING ON, PAVE ANOTHER."

I KNEW IT WAS TIME TO BE ON MY OWN. I WANTED MORE. I WANTED HOLLYWOOD.

AFTER PORTER, I TOURED A BIT WITH MY "TRAVELING FAMILY BAND." MY FAMILY HAD GROWN UP SINGING AND PLAYING MUSIC, SO WHY NOT?

Dolly

THAT ENDED IN 1976. BY THEN, I'D CREATED A PUBLISHING COMPANY AND STARTED ENTERTAINING THE IDEA OF BEIN' A MOVIE STAR. MY VARIETY SHOW, DOLLY, WAS BORN.

LADIES AND GENTLEMEN! MIS DOLLY PARTON

THE SHOW OPENED EACH WEEK WITH A CLOSE-UP ON A BUTTERFLY MADE OF LIGHT PERCHED ATOP MY NAME. THE CAMERA WOULD PULL BACK, REVEALING MY NAME. I'D GLIDE INTO THE FRAME ON A VELVET ROPE SWING AS RALPH EMERY, OUR ANNOUNCER, SAID:

AND THEN I'D SING. IT WAS ALL VERY 1970'S.

THE SHOW WAS THE MOST EXPENSIVE SHOW EVER AIRED. IT COST $100,000 AN EPISODE AND ATTRACTED SINGERS LIKE EMMYLOU HARRIS, LINDA RONDSTADT, AND MARILYN MCCOO. IT WAS ALL REAL FANCY.

WE PULLED IN 9 MILLION VIEWERS A WEEK. NOT TOO SHABBY.

BUT IT WASN'T ENOUGH FOR ME. I PULLED THE PLUG AND THE STUDIO CITED IT AS "CREATIVE DIFFERENCES."

IN 1980, THINGS REALLY GOT CRAZY FOR ME.

NO, I CAN'T I'M JUST... TIRED, JANE.

9 to 5

LILY, PATRICIA RESNICK WROTE THE ROLE OF VIOLET NEWSTEAD WITH YOU IN MIND.

THEY'LL FIND SOMEONE ELSE. CAROL BURNETT OR SOMEONE. I'VE BEEN SHOOTING FOR SEVEN MONTHS –

THE INCREDIBLE SHRINKING WOMAN WAS –

A CHORE, JANE. I'VE MADE UP MY MIND.

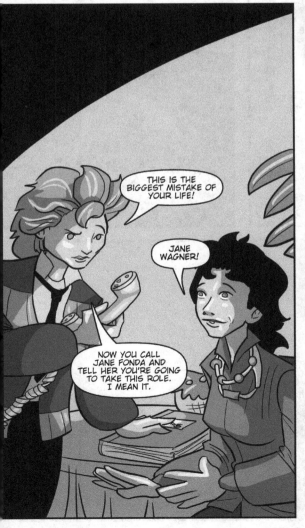

THIS IS THE BIGGEST MISTAKE OF YOUR LIFE!

JANE WAGNER!

NOW YOU CALL JANE FONDA AND TELL HER YOU'RE GOING TO TAKE THIS ROLE. I MEAN IT.

FINE, IF IT MEANS THAT MUCH TO YOU.

THE FILM STARS THREE WOMEN. I WONDER WHO THEY HAVE IN MIND FOR THE THIRD PERSON?

DOIN' 9 TO 5 WAS A GREAT DECISION, BOTH PERSONALLY AND PROFESSIONALLY. I MADE SOME LIFELONG FRIENDS, MADE A STATEMENT ABOUT WOMEN'S RIGHTS, AND RECEIVED AN OSCAR NOMINATION FOR WRITING THE TITLE SONG AND TWO GRAMMY AWARDS FOR BEST COUNTRY SONG AND BEST FEMALE COUNTRY VOCAL PERFORMANCE.

I KNOW WHO I AM. I KNOW WHAT I CAN AND CAN'T DO. I KNOW WHAT I WILL AND WON'T DO. I KNOW WHAT I AM CAPABLE OF AND I DON'T AGREE TO DO THINGS THAT I DON'T THINK I CAN PULL OFF.

SO IT WAS A NATURAL FIT FOR ME TO DO THE SCREEN VERSION OF BEST LITTLE WHOREHOUSE IN 1982.

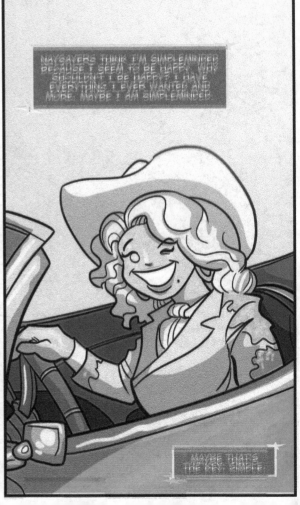

NAYSAYERS THINK I'M SIMPLEMINDED BECAUSE I SEEM TO BE HAPPY. WHY SHOULDN'T I BE HAPPY? I HAVE EVERYTHING I EVER WANTED AND MORE. MAYBE I AM SIMPLEMINDED.

MAYBE THAT'S THE KEY. SIMPLE.

THAT REMINDS ME OF THE TIME I ALMOST QUIT MAKIN' MOVIES THANKS TO THE 1992 FILM, STRAIGHT TALK.

THE CHARACTER, SHIRLEE, WAS SO ME THAT I DIDN'T REALLY FEEL LIKE I WAS ACTING, BUT OF COURSE, I HAD TO GO DEEP INSIDE AND I HAD A GREAT DIRECTOR.

IF I WAS TRYING TOO HARD TO DO IT MY WAY, HE WAS WONDERFUL TO SAY,

WELL, YOU NEED TO HAVE A LITTLE MORE EDGE.

BUT HE LIKED ME BEING MY OWN THING, BEING MY OWN SELF AS MUCH AS I COULD, SO I DIDN'T FEEL LIKE I WAS REALLY ACTING THAT MUCH. THAT WORRIED ME, OF COURSE.

IT WAS MY FIRST LEAD, I THINK I WAS TRYIN' TOO HARD. THE FILM RECEIVED LUKEWARM REVIEWS BUT DID HAVE SOME REDEEMING MOMENTS.

I PLAYED A RADIO HOST WHO SHOT STRAIGHT WITH MY ADVICE. IN ONE SCENE, A CALLER IS STRUGGLING WITH THE DECISION TO BECOME TRANSGENDER. I GOT TO SAY,

IF YOU'RE SURE THAT'S WHAT YOU REALLY WANT, ALL I CAN SAY IS DON'T TRY TO PERM YOUR OWN HAIR AND DON'T WEAR HIGH HEELS ON A SOGGY LAWN!

YOU RECENTLY THREW SUPPORT TO THE LGBT COMMUNITY...

OH, I'M ALWAYS ENCOURAGING - WELL, I'M NOT ENCOURAGING - THEY MADE ME THE POSTER CHILD I THINK BECAUSE I'M SO OUTSPOKEN AS BEING ACCEPTING OF PEOPLE IN GENERAL. WE ARE ALL GOD'S CHILDREN.

I'VE OFTEN SAID PEOPLE DON'T COME TO SEE ME TO SEE ME, THEY COME TO SEE ME TO SEE THEM.

Michael Frizell ————————————— Writer

Ramon Salas ————————————— Art

Benjamin Glibert ————————————— Letters

Darren G. Davis ————————————— Editor

Dave Ryan ————————————— Cover

Cover B: Ramon Salas

Darren G. Davis
Publisher

Maggie Jessup
Publicity

Susan Ferris
Entertainment Manager

CPSIA information can be obtained
at www.ICGtesting.com
Printed in the USA
LVHW061505250321
682333LV00026B/24